the cloning

also by peter wild

Collections

Limited Editions

the cloning

by Peter Wild

Doubleday & Company, Inc.
Garden City, New York
1974

10/1974
Am Lit

Some of these poems first appeared in publications: PIL-
GRIMS, HISTORY OF THE HORSE, IN CALIFORNIA,
North American Review, Copyright © 1973 by The Univer-
sity of Northern Iowa, and THE BUFFALO, *North Amer-
ican Review,* Copyright © 1972 by The University of North-
ern Iowa; WARRIOR, *The Sou'wester,* Copyright © 1973 by
The Board of Trustees of Southern Illinois University at Ed-
wardsville; SUN, *Prairie Schooner,* Copyright © 1973 by the
University of Nebraska Press; BAMBOO, FOR THE SIERRA
CLUB, *Buffalo,* Copyright © 1973 by Buffalo Press; NOAH,
Merrill Poetry Quarterly; MEAT LOAF, THE ACOLYTE,
TUMACACORI, POEM FOR LEE OLER, in book TUMA-
CACORI, published by Twowindows Press; VICTOR, in
book THE SENSUOUS PRESIDENT BY "K", New Rivers
Press, Copyright © 1973 by New Rivers Press; A PASSING
ILLNESS, *Folio,* Copyright © 1973 by Adele Sophie de la
Barre; RESOLUTION and WOMAN, *The Falcon,* Copyright
© 1972, 1973 by Mansfield State College, respectively; VIO-
LENCE, *Noise Quarterly;* ADVICE, DISK, *Granite,* Copy-
right © 1974 by Granite Publications; FOR HENRY
BESTON, *Cafeteria,* Copyright © 1973 by Cafeteria; CON-
DITION, *Lillabulero,* Copyright © 1974 by Lillabulero Press;
MESCAL MTNS., *Chicago Review,* Copyright © 1973 by
Chicago Review; THE WILDERNESS, *Wind;* SILVERBELL,
DIVORCEE, *The New Newspaper;* THE HOLE, *Foxfire,*
Copyright © 1974 by The Foxfire Fund, Inc.; THE PROPA-
GANDIST, *Gulfstream,* Copyright © 1973 by GULF-
STREAM Press; ESKIMOS, *Poiesis;* THE ESKIMO MASK,
Minnesota Review, Copyright © 1972 by New Rivers Press;
OPTION, TWINS, *Seneca Review,* Copyright © 1972, 1974
by Hobart & William Smith Student Assn., respectively;
STEAKBONES, *The Little Magazine,* Copyright © 1973 by
The Little Magazine; TERMITES, *Mademoiselle.*

Library of Congress Cataloging in Publication Data
Wild, Peter.
The Cloning.
Poems.
I. Title.
PS3573.I42C5   811'.5'4
ISBN 0-385-07595-2 Trade
0-385-07591-X Paperbound
Library of Congress Catalog Card Number 74–131
Copyright © 1973, 1974 by PETER WILD
Printed in the United States of America
First Edition

For Buzz and Mary Anne

contents

Friday Groupers

Steakbones

the cloning

Friday Groupers

Dakotas

He rides with his wife's
        stove tied to his saddle
    a gold-plated charm
long loaves of bread
        tucked up his sleeves,
    sticking like teeth from his hat
  that remind him of her wrists.
all those days
        that pass like hours
    the land dangling under his feet.
once he sees a train
        the good luck of the future
                speeding across a lake
        where there is no lake
and further into the brittle days
        that spurt around his horse's feet
    a calf, a shadow that runs up
                            its new trail
        following a voice into the rocks,
bawling is sucked into the cave,
        that windy hole, an intestine where
    a hundred years later others
slither in rubber suits,
        candles anchored in their heads.

Here and there we see the cars
of tourists parked off the road.
further, past Oracle, on
the high plains there are more
of them, shiny sedans, campers,
station wagons scattered
to left and right, hub-deep
in rabbit grass, parked under the mimosas.
outside the children dance in their jumpers
waiting to talk to the stern Indians,
to watch as the icy snakes of the streams
that shoot out of the sand hills
plunge through their hands like cold lightning. nearby
their fathers stand frowning, then
turn to their wives, and growing
new skins much like the old ones
but brighter the families sail
off in chains smiling as the mountains open
into a sky white as their teeth, as their wings.

Pilgrims

Under the stars
the turtle closes her eyes.
her lids fall,
embroidered shades
coming down around a house
and continue, the skeletal legs
of a horse, silver wax
dripping through the darkness toward the ground.
only once her plates glow,
light around the doors
of vaults, and then go out.
her tail switches
    where the night starts
and her mouth where the foaming day
begins for someone else.
meanwhile in the forest
they lay themselves down
this is their night only
and they grapple, wrapping
themselves in their limbs,
staring into the mockery of ashes,
skirts, the belly of a cow ripped out,
feel their legs below,
                cold cordwood,
watching where their leather vests
open, the growing pyramids
of snow pile out, high among the foliage
the pinpoints forming,
the flaming words begin to fall.

For Buzz and Mary Anne

At the end of the trail
with your wife, sticks
halo and perfume
you pass the boiler of a locomotive
glutted with ice cream
                    dying among the rocks,
and further over the cracked boulders
find your last neighbor
gimpy, under five feet,
weeping over his blackened dahlia bulbs,
his mildewed dog, as he
turns away from the new ones
you both bring in a box
and beyond the dead valley
the Sawtooth Range as you
say in a letter riding into
the showers in greys, pinks and blues.

Like the rest of us
the sun has his children
but they are blind sheep
with eyes small as beetle eyes.
by day he sends them into a cave
to protect them from the light;
in the doorway they jump over his finger.
in there they raise up their arms, sing hymns
some moan or play checkers.
while out at sea a wave comes
raised up like a mad chicken or a prophet
running in his skirts across the sea,
his hair curling into eyes and fingers.

Dreams

It is the time of year to climb into the tree
my wife, her lap a pool of sky and leaves,
tells me not to do it, that the trees
                         have a life to themselves
    but I go, urged by the plumber across the street
      who has told me how to put them in shape,
of the dangers of rot when dirt
                         blows in between the joints.
he watches from the window
          as slinging a saw I tread up the ladder,
    leave it and climb through the branches.
below the world is a pearl sea
                              of clouds and voices
          and I can hear him beneath
      pointing where I might be to his wife with the
                         green synthetic-emerald ring.
up here the trunks of the mulberry
      flower even further, smooth as the limbs of a girl
          to which I cling.
      not knowing the parts
                    I cut at a few.
          far beyond surprise
    they shudder then dive toward the mists
              below with a terrible lack of thunder.
shaken, I come down much later,
      leaving the stubs to heal in the ether.
          in the kitchen stuff myself with ice cream.

Bamboo

If you feed it enough
it will grow
like some beast out there
springing from the ground,
putting on clothes and claws
of fire.

on Tuesday morning
with nothing to do
but be correct beneath the
glaucous sky, a white sheet sail
pressing us, I let
the water run for hours

through the hose, drawing
its constant whisper from the house.
and at noon remembering go out
to see it, already speckled,
one leg lifted, tongues
split, eyeing the clouds.

Warrior

At times he remembers
waking in the middle of the night
dancing into sleep in the daylight,
the hole in his ankle among feathers,
the inset: mountains and a stream,
that rose, liquid in a tube
up his legs on its own power,
the jewels far out falling from
his wrists and fingers, until
it shot from his mouth,
a solid stream of light. eyes
encrusted he looked down
the hole of his throat
and saw the white geese, the
occasional thatched roofs of the peasants,
the land passing below
which now and then showed
the nail of a toe, a vein, the color, the
shape of a foot following.

Meat Loaf

All the beasts that went into it
come out, the painted tin dove, enamel
beak floating upright in the soup,
the buffalo with haunches grinding.
even my dog swims up, offers
a badly written poem from her mouth.
a white finger, rusted scissors, a bandage.

      to survive red lights in the rain
or the policemen with white belts
          and pistols standing under them.

I know somewhere to the south across deserts
      a bleating Arab is selling honey cakes,
   brother to the palms, in that light
      feathers of iron with eyes behind him.

but the coal barges slip away from their embrace
     and begin revolving slowly down the river Main
  the wild rice jumps up
and runs screaming on dirty legs back to the swamp.

You had the distinction
        of being the crazyman of the neighborhood.
      what with the wickedness,
             the sky moving over the land,
you had to drink alone.

all those cubits,
                    the nails in piles—
    they built themselves
   like words over the years
        working toward a metaphor.

until
        below your face followed
           day by day in the rotten water.
you got off
     milked your cows,
  felt the wine rising warm in the vines.

The Hearing

The stars have walked down off the mountain
and stroll around your back yard
                        through the aspens, past the guest house
holding each others' thin hands.
this is the promise we bring to you
                                    buoyed on one hip,
a loaf of bread big as a car
our uncounted children crawl through.
at night we gather in the living room
                            and make intimate plans
to save the forest, while your daughter plays sonatas.
like crystals they exude from the
                        polished stumps of your knees
and light around your head,
                        mosquitoes held by your hands.
toward midnight the earth
                takes one sliding step forward.
and as we go to bed, out in the cienaga
            the beavers, newly come, nose
        into the lake like two shoes,
    the same I almost step on the next
morning eyeing me from the grass, come to life again.

There is a fence in your stomach
on the pickets hang dead crows, bits of flesh
no, they are more like girls,
                              skin turned black by the sun,
      eyes pebbles in their sockets.
and that is why when your hands go there
          by mistake for something to eat
and your mouth opens unawares
          lifting in the deep-frozen steaks, ballerina's
    legs past the rays
                              rushing from your throat
the birds appear again in your eyes
            flying low and heavy over the swamps
      drugged, looking this way and that
flapping their bootblack wings.

Termites

The termites climb from the earth
which is their Bible. like us
they are convinced
they are Adam. and make tubes
of trees, a night branching
through a night following their paths.
that dense sky, the bread
they never break through,
is always just ahead:
more ravenous
they lick against the skin
of that other lighter world.

A Passing Illness

Those good citizens the clouds
            go over without sickness,
    frogstroking toward their dreams
              with a passionless health.
and you having risen
          pale from your death at the proper hour
    to do the shopping, to send the dirt of our wash
               sucking through the city's system—
hearing the cars go by all day
        I throw off a week of books,
    stand out by the woodpile in the sun
            with my wool cap on
          slicing the logs into shadows.
        the axe falls, a bit of sunlight through my hands.
and you come home like a Lazarus
             not knowing the difference,
       tidy up the house.
that night the guests
        mumble like fathers in the next room
           talking about their children,
later come in a group to stand around
        the bed with sweating iridescent faces
    and mouths that tear when they whisper.

Gandhi said that the earth
was surrounded by a thin shell
of heaven, like the inside of an egg
and said that if you could
burst through your head like a yellow rocket
hearing the sound tanks
would rush together firing
from all their portholes,
buildings would kiss.
up there the earth
below veined like an embryo
he felt at last he had no tongue. peasants
flew like birds or chains from his wrists.
just leaving
looking down he saw his sandals
filled with copper ants. propelled,
behind he heard his skeleton making sucking sounds.

The Acolyte

What is new to you
is new to others
the monk paralyzed eating bread
and the fire appearing after noon
like statues one by one in the bays of the arcade.
once she starts running
she can go anywhere
bent over her hoop, you can
see her kidneys boiling just under the skin.
and over your shoulder
her face there about to scream
holding a rusted flintlock;
on chilly nights a metal
cock perched on a spire
beginning to wrinkle as if
to burn, to burst into chocolate.
we have told this story
for every reason.
still the owl in his tree sucks up birds
and after one glass of it the locomotive
begins crossing his valley
where the murdered girls
           drag their feet.

Violence

Atop your house is another
shaped like a chimney,
a little stucco hut with red tiles.
in the wind it moves like a willow,
a woman weeping, clasping her hands.
in the still afternoons saints pop
from the windows playing their flutes,
grab at their hats, rainbow
halos made of sticks.

out riding on your bicycle
your legs go round and round
made of colored flesh, the wreckage
and sunlight on the silt at the
mouths of shifting rivers. your head
a piece of dung with
gold glasses on a white thistle.
out on the deserts drinking juice,
at noon sitting on mountains, your haunches
eating the rocks, or through neighborhoods
while men labor on their lawns, with your pack on
pulling the whole robed world behind you,
your halter unties itself, Pullmans
shoot off to fly through the clouds,
revealing where your breasts were
the caves, two trees torn out, the tangled roots.

Tumacacori

It takes us years to get there
the mountains splitting at our steps
and when we do we are old,
the waterdogs at your breasts are stars
wagging their tails to the juices,
you slump all flesh in your transparent clothes.
and I—still holding the staff
that wrinkles, stabbing my toes,
chasing away the iron bits of flies,
        gold legs and parts of jewels—
                        don't know where we were.
behind the cinder hills the moon
                        shoots out like a hot clay puppy
and then explodes.
                        but there is the tavern
again, at our steps rising from the ground, the same
we read about, with its ancient soldiers
combing their beards as they pass behind
                        the crenels,
waxed and perfumed, reciting lines we can almost read
                        on their halberds.
they point the other way,
almost touching your cloudy shoulder,
and though inside we see the yellow faces
washed like trees against the bar, their bulbous
                        pistols,
hear their jokes around the spinning girl,
go down like water this time over stone,
                        through the stinking foliage,
to the mud flats, daylight along the cloth
of the river, where the Pimas labor, as they
                        have always labored,

knee-deep, frog-mouthed, bending into the steam.
with your finger you cut a path across the skin,
wiping off the beads of words, delighted taste it.
in horror I draw back. but though eyeing
you once, looking up your rainbow skirts,
the women stand speechless, vomit onions,
                                    they hardly notice.
weary, you take my hand to the garden
where all the signs have pointed
and find the place as if prepared, with
the towel and toothbrush laid out, the venous fountain,
the gnomish olives. you lift your hair off
and I beside you on the bench, chest
gone to wood, awkward as I am bend,
lay my head past the red hard-rubber nubs
into the two ribs of your arms where you cradle
it singing, and I sleepless
watch the daylight stars
going over like burning mites
                        above your moth breath.

Advice

Make sure your windows open
into your neighbor's yard
        where there is no one home,
so that at the first big step
      snaking your leg out you will plunge
    up to the waist in salty foam.
across the street all night the dog howls
        in the chimney, and the people
     visiting next door stare in their gowns at your
ghost tearing around the house
        as their teeth crack out like flowers, as
              their fingers crush the sills.
avoid incest: keep your rakes
      locked in the cellar, in the refrigerator
        an extra quart of milk, half full;
fire smoulders, then spreads into a gaseous ball
     like the wind fondling the hairy leg
                of your mistress.
to be safe, stay close to the floor,
      hang a sheet out with your blood type
   and position
      smeared in large Chinese characters for rescue.
enter the fire.
      while you're waiting for the horn,
    the giant to mount your roof, chop a hole,
             blare through,
picking your nose search under
       the beds for the children's dolls,
    scratch a message in the floor with one toe.
but if you must escape
     first stand up, un-
       hitching your desire, put your hand
  against the door like a breast,
enter the fire.

For Henry Beston

I

The waves twirl in
    a paper plate.
from far off it curves,
       the pinhead of a swimmer.
but landing at his feet
    sees his name written
  in large Turkish letters
          with a Flair pen.
and looking up to the east, over the sea
          a vision of Turkey rising.

II

In the yellow noon
       helicopters fly high
   and north, lines out dragging behind.
he slouches in the sound of the surf
       writing it in his notebook,
while inland over the moors
    a deer stands with her chin up bristling
         over the ice floes.

III

At night he notices a hole in his sock
       but hangs them up for breakfast
    and puts a bun out for the Nauset guard.
a steamer passes his window
       and plows into the dunes,

the same he will see weeks later
      backing out of the sand after a storm,
   returning from its voyage, a wreck
        with smiling Chinamen on it
          and the groans of birds inside,
skidding south on its flank past him
            through the surf in the moonlight.

Condition

Chekhov understood
that when you turn the peasants loose
with axes in the woods their heads
become moons, and they
cut the forests down,
in sheer pleasure shuffle home drunk
and laying their globes on the wooden
tables, from one side of the mouth call for their
suppers, then rape the women on the floor.
every day above them the sky tears a little.
the middle class becomes sausages.
that those others, whose arms
are infinitely small caliber pistols,
thinking of their treasure lose it
saving their souls. they with their
underfed women, who when they can't
breathe, run hysterically through the upstairs
rooms, bumping into one another, eating perfume, so that
the whole house tilts. some
dance and prepare for war. above
a fierce God calls, and those others
run into the streets making fools of themselves, then
travel seeing it on trains in faces,
the women who lunge toward them
as if on fire, eyes eggs, tearing at their breasts;
the meals, the delicate buildings that
take fire at the touch, and in their hands
when they dare look see the forests
growing again, running up their arms like escaping insects.

Mescal Mtns.

Sometimes, by swallowing, you can
tell men are cows,
how they go over the three mountains
                              on five wooden legs,
on soft toes and bulbous calluses,
their snouts berries burning toward the clouds.
all day facing the peaks to the west, snow
crooking in the sun, you go down
with the others, fingers lining your stomach,
denying horizons over the warm rocks, your life
at the ends of the stretching intestines of your arms
until at the bottom sitting where
the sand is water you want to go up,
swim past the scratched ledges, take
the whole thing at noon in your mouth.
far away Winkelman, a mound of Kleenex,
sticks in its crotch, miners in bars, the girls'
legs like French fries falling out,
but by the time you labor to the top
the frog legs are circling in your cold pockets,
the peaks harden against the sky,
and ahead the lights in the pit are twinkling on as
behind where you came out the muscular teeth
are leaning toward their colors into the jaw.
and riding home through the burnt mountains
                              beneath the grinning stars
you see yourself, upright with the others, molars
in another mouth by the lights of the passing cars.

Good Luck

The birds fly through the
                sky carrying their wooden signs
        behind one cloud opens
    into an eye, that blushes shut
                    and covers itself with hair.
and while they have passed
                into their own time
        red moon:
                        night on the tarry lake
        in yours walking home
far past noon into the cold
        you find a girl, a grey leaf
                in the gutter, marbles for eyes.
when you stoop to open
        the flimsy door in her chest
        a door to an old attic
it is there again
        defined on her guts bulging toward you,
    the sky with its cirrus tails,
the ducks, mouths edged with gold
                pursuing their paths on the upturned
            knifeblades of air on which they fly.

The Wilderness

At our fingertips the world
lies tottering in its shapes,
chunks of beef piled in blocks,
leftovers sliding off, a bone
sticking from a peak, beards
flowing from the cliffs.
standing before it how
are we armed for this.
muscle growing lean in our shirts,
living at the ends of our whiskers.
on your hip the egg of your
canteen breaks, a hairy yolk
veins down your chewed leg—a land
that changes colors in the wind, running
off in waves behind its dancing bears

                              to a smooth horizon
wondrous and innocent and cool as the moon.
at your boot I see where lightning
has struck, and in the pit
oozing from the wound a hardened

                                    tip of chalcedony.
but behind us already the trailers
are moving up the slopes among the cactus
bearing their retirees, and out of the distance
the living crawling bones of the city. nearby
the cows cling bellowing, legs
drawn up into the mesquites. you
look back at me with the
eyes of some mad saint, moving
the fish flesh of your lips, the disease
of the sky spreading across your cheeks. . . .

Friday Groupers

The fish bubbles in the hairy mouth
and we lie back in our jackets
feet propped to its yellow words
against a night closing down
with the kind of clouds you might paint
on a bad day. Dozer tears into the shadows
after his tennis ball.
jabbing at the bacon you talk
about the young and their beautiful bodies,
how you were gassed in Tennessee.
later, inside with the women
                         beneath a light that is
only a semblance of light on the oak table,
tell us about your daughter, twelve
feet tall and bulletproof
in San Diego, how when she speaks
for the Maharishi a great
                         wind of hair blows out.
nearsighted we strain toward your work,
colored feet walking across the frames.
in a night too cold for sandals
walk home from your lighted ship,
                         past the morays of the houses.
to the west the clouds
have indeed eaten the mountains
as the wind nuzzles up our pant holes,
lie there in their places,
bloated fish at the bottom of a sea
waiting for morning, when the hills
will return marching in their veils, restore
themselves with the hours, and expanding with
the day will rise, lightly fly away
as the sunny stars pass over.

Distrust

Turning it over again
feeding the birds
my wife flying from the house
like a tongue from a mouth
and the two lying on the corner
fallen from the sky.
barefoot in the cold she squats by one
and holds her down by the shoulder,
screaming at the twisting arms,
the thing at the back of her head
flowing around her face. I
pass the boy who hangs from his key
then falls from the truck, gets up
and falls again, and eyeing
the broken cedar trunks crawl
through the neighbor's scratchy hedge—
the ground clean, he has even
raked there—to touch the girl's cold
fleshy back where the shirt is torn
as if to wake her up. closer
her eyes are shut at the twisted roots,
her lips blue, and breathing down
on her see the blood from her mouth
bunching on the swept earth,
as if next day standing at the feeder
again in my wool cap while
above the finches and the pigeons huddle
on the branches in the bare November sunset
words had anything to do with it.

After Rain

When you go out
down the wooden steps
fresh as omelets, the
morning like a greedy hunchback
running away, the sun
cutting into one shoulder.
behind last night's dough
still struggles in the bowl
growing fragile arms and
little fish mouths allover. under
the tejido your mother prays
for your brother eating candles,
your father's pipes cold on the shelf.
your flesh falling into each shoe,
a brown jelly around the bones
and the belly's black mouth
licking up toward the breasts,
that rise around the neck,
                              threaten to spill out.
but this has all been taken care of.
past the white flagpole your purse
hangs from your shoulder heavy
with books, and beyond the city
up close now with its blank windows,
the buildings that you touch, the mountains fawn,
young dogs tasting their teeth with their tongues,
envious of puddles.

Silverbell

You can hold it
if you don't move,
a corolla of ash
there beneath your hat

like some girl in a picture
whose smile slides
halfway across the film,
her teeth a white belt.

there beyond the frayed
blunt ends of your boots
returned to their colors, two
ships at last beached on land

you remember the effluent, shacks,
dragon food beneath the mountains,
and the girls breathing through the
blouses you see through,

smiling at the postmaster
who celebrates, handing out
his blazing stamps.

Steakbones

Steakbones

My neighbor puts steakbones
under his trees.
walking in the alley, there he is
this bishop of the church in his robe
and slippers, holding a lamp
like the sage on Hills Brothers Coffee
stooping, turning them over with a rake
because they are growing hair.
he spends evenings dozing
on the back porch chasing the dogs away
that sail back and forth over the fence.
on weekends lets his grandchildren
play with them, use them as boomerangs,
as parts for their airplanes. but when
they go home he makes them put them back
each to its own rounded place,
rotting eggs into their nests, like
loaded pistols back into their cases. I have read
that after years if the mice don't get them,
the ants carry them away, they begin to disintegrate,
a constant phosphorous rain like uranium
penetrating the soil. meanwhile they lie there
in their wild beards, some with lipstick smiles
on their faces, others growing the thin vestigial
legs of lizards, glowing in their circles,
humming their own private music
as above the citrus leaves curl turning a violent green
putting out their globing fruit, and he
lies awake on his back beneath his vandyke,
ripening overnight in anticipation.

Woman

Out on the beach you begin undressing
unfortunately all your reasons are good ones.
milk falls from your breasts as you stoop,
                              making oblong arcs across the sand.
your eyes are circles.
by now nothing can save your reputation.
and walk away buttocks
                    drooping, moving in their silver foil.
once in you are a skeleton
                              buoyed by salt.
my hands fly before my face like shadows,
                                    like black bacon.
but you rise up once before sinking, a torso
                    turning landward your burnt-out Janus face,
your breasts are holes, your eyes caves,
and howl.
far out I see a wave, a little man
                                    in a coat
skipping across the water toward you.

We have a few victories
but many defeats
at night when we sit on our wooden chairs
with our skinny violated sisters
their vaginas hang to the floor
like the dry moss on tropical trees.
we know their every secret.
when we swallow, coffee spurts
over us like hair from our ears. they
move their hands to our knees.
still there are the forests out there
growing on starlight
from the rocks giving birth.
they comb our hair
miraculously we eat.
and each morning backs fresh the clouds
travel past like the years
with their celebrations,
dragons snorting, mad glass babies
through whose skin we see
the curling minute functions, hungry
someday to eat the earth.

Twins

Released from their pillars
the priests fly toward one another,
two sorrowing women
baring their teeth.
their clothes are stars
their hands out front brooms.
they speak the same language
they eat the same food,
and when they collide
it is like the two shores
of a continent coming together,
an omelet folded on itself.
sparks fly from their ears,
their teeth lock in the
embrace of lovers,
fuselage embedded in fuselage,
                    all night whispering
to each other the same
                  comfortable story.

Divorcee

When I am away from you
        I am totally destroyed, a stick man
watching his ribs like the seasons
        falling in upon their smoke
and although all day I have climbed
        behind the marvelous divorcee
  with her lunch on my back
climbing hand over hand on the
     silver branches of the oaks
lifting ourselves out of the morning
   shadows, with the others scrambling at last
        on all sides up the peak
coming home she drives too fast
      talking about her husband, the miners
released for the weekend show their
       gold teeth speeding past.
I slump studying maps
       eating cookies across the expanding land,
  the weekend light leaping through my fingers
              eating at my knees,
until we come to the familiar river of sand
       choked with its flowing crosses, the
    lion content gnawing his hill
remembering the mail stacked
         in corners around the house
   and you in bed with the dog
       watching the pictures in your teeth,
stumble in to sit a fire on my lips
         half the night in the back yard
    drinking beer beneath the trees
   holding their stars and sleeping birds
who wake off and on
     to look around in the dark
   then go back to sleep.

History of the Horse

When the first horses came
they were wooden skeletons
stumbling sheepishly out of
the gravelly sunrise. we
picked the flesh from
their bones, the fire strips from
their eyes and ribs, and
with the other garbage
kicked the rest over the cliffs.
but our women glued buckskin
to their legs, and in their ears
hung trinkets. mornings they
came up to our tents smiling
like second moons, and we rode them
who could take us on their thoughts
over the ranges, and when they dropped
found their flesh delicious. we
clothed them in the robes from our backs,
made gold plugs for their noses
and they eating the grass up as in
some dream increased, grew
strong, large as armed windmills
spinning in the sun. released
they flew like lions over the hills
to pounce on mountains, claws spread. we
took their children in, built stone houses for them,
fed them incense, fruit, on holy days
presented the silent virgin's flesh.
at night our village is an island
surrounded by their moving lights
and screams as they tear up the earth
and we sleep in our tattered tents
hugging the tiny scapulas of the
                        sacrifice on which we dream.

In California under the shadow
of the Sierra the wine
bubbles out of the ground,
a hot foam squeezed between
faults, from the pressure
of thermal oceans
under the bending land.
there the girls, air
wrapped in red bandannas
bend to pick the nuggets
from the lava earth
with fingers that echo
their brown breasts
swinging forward in their shirts.
all afternoon the men lounge
high on oaken cart wheels,
take the wind in their teeth,
spit, and bound thin in their
white sashes watch them.
toward evening along the ridge rocks
the cedars burn, reflected
in the lakes of loam; the
planes land, the trains
grind to a halt outside town.
going home they shake the juice
from their fingers, drip by
drip from the skins to the tube.
the planes rise, the trains
wind off into the cooling night
following their burning heads
through the pines, becoming more silent.
it plunges, a cascade under
the night of the land,

strains up mountains,
rushing down slopes
grows a froth tinged
with the moon under the snow,
spreads over the plains,
through the veins of a hand.
already it is next day in the same land
and offshore from Louisiana the
sea bulges, an eye
pokes out, the pig-
creature born again
in his fat of salt and
garbage swims toward the land
as back through the stars
they dance in their cottages
slicing their breasts, making
wreaths of the furniture,
uncorks the nipple, hangs there.

The Hole

Caliche is the belly
               of the sky
turned over,
an innocent turtle
            wiggling on its back
that I eat with a pick
                 and my spine.
    after the season the tribes
have gathered in the swales
      and stay awake all night
          growing lean and light-headed
                   dreaming of buffalo
       listening to the sounds of the
                  night music
     in the low places, through the long grass.
down there I am at peace
but out in the daylight
      it is another thing
          a space for someone
   to step into
              a drunk
      going down like a windmill,
an old lady
      weeping before a jury
   for my skin.
but I think of all the trees out there
          crowded in nurseries
        the Aleppo pines in five
     seven and fifteen gallon cans
eager to run into it
     like the opening of Oklahoma
  fill it up,
   try their hands at the sky.

The Buffalo

I have opened my eyes a thousand times
to the sound of falling snow, like a puppy born
to light, and seen the buffalo falling,
a rainbow in cascade over the cartilaginous brow
of a cloud moving across the land

and my ears opened, new wax
to the pleasant music of their
floating down, stiff-legged
howling, their lips gold
and then up again through the earth
and charging through a mountain

when you go to the spot and press
the ground, dampness and grass,
there is nothing there except
what you can imagine before
your receding toes. your breath makes no sound.

and a party comes dancing with
its lamps and furniture, under tables,
out, speaking in a language
that you understand before you know. the girls'
white flesh soft as codfish
as they take your arm becomes your own.

still after they have gone, constantly
changing clothes, you see them on the horizon
and they have grown to millions singing
in their new robes. still you are in your shoes
and under your tongue something melting like a coin.

you go back to find the wet seam
of the wound. your heart grows big
as your feet go cold. and stooped there,
pierced with arrows, they swirl back
moving their lips in and out, wearing horns,
reaching for the sunset that snakes and twists
                              in your bowels.

The Ranger

Before his eyes the vitamins
        pour out of the ground
    like heat, like chips of wood
  that pierce his ears, fly
          past him to perch in the trees

up here on the plateau where
            on warm days
    the clouds come down from the sky,
  crowd toward him through the pines
               like friendly sheep
and at night the cold nuzzles in his hair,
              a nest out of reach

he is a guardian, a priest.
    looking at his pitch hands
   he knows his waist could turn
 into pools of fire
      preceding him at noon over the meadows
    that in the dark he could become
   a bear losing his eyes, the top of his head
    to towers of smoking oil

when he gets home
    before opening his letters
  he drops the bulbs of his guns
           into a chair
in a quiet voice tells his wife
      all the old secret stories,
   who seeing his teeth drip
 forgetting supper flees to her bed where
    he cuts her to pieces with an axe;

next Saturday goes to town
  where the farmers are fixing their wagons,
    whose faces are wrinkled
      much like his, who wink at him.

The Burglar

If I could wrap you
               in a cocoon of myth
and light,
               the thief in his cave
        pinched at the waist,
who comes out once a year,
               lifting his knees high
        around the corner of my house,
                    softly above the frosted leaves
                        curled in the October moonlight,
       the knot of fire
          at the center of my heavy heart his desire,
but the dog will have no truck with it,
   at three in the morning
             gallops round and round the house
       snarling at each door
               to devour the monster,
and I, still half in my dreams
       wake, sit upright
into the great bloom
       of the flashlight,
where you witness
          full of fright
      a half-naked bearded man
rising to the window
       from the black sea of the room.
dumbstruck I fall back
       like a tongue into its mouth
     quivering at the roots,
and hear your footsteps clattering
          off into the moonlit depths of the neighborhood,
        dropping your pipe,
cursing, tearing your clothes on the bushes.

Disk

Men who have slipped disks stand
a baby being born from their hips
the history they carry
offered like cigars
to friends digging holes
walking across their yards with trees.

                              under the knife
they saw far beyond the light
birds growing, hair from a swampy
sun, and now the insulting patterns
of doilies, imperfect beneath their hands.
when the sun goes down all things human rest
but they must get up, do witness
beneath the liquid oblong moon, stumble
on the dog doubled
on his spine biting a flea.

The Propagandist

Behind you
is what you have always wanted
a landscape with a moon
and a set of fingers

before him
the shepherd drives his three tiny sheep
with just a touch, a gesture,
                    a puff from a straw

while the cow comes floating along,
                              a burlap mountain,
                    absorbs them.
          after an hour they fall from her tongue
                         the light of her mouth,
and she gazes back insulted.

you have always known, in your weary hours,
               when your ears are folded in your lap
          like laundered shirts,
     that your mother is a stone, flesh
                              married to a cushion,
               and she goes sailing over, throwing out clusters
                    of potatoes for punishment

that when you breathe you can blow
                    the limbs from pines, then the bark,
                              leaving whole forests
          standing, naked emasculated boys.
that at your glance the water closes its eyes
                    and crawls back toward the rock.

a wind of birds that are nails
                    following the shapes of the earth,
                         setting fire to cabins.

a river of air scouring contours,
　　　　　that whirls and screams and
　　　　　　　　disappears far out in the smooth
　　　　　　　　fissures of the desert. . . .

Eskimos

At night the Eskimos stretch out next to the dead whale
their faces moons in ragged hair,
    legs their sons following behind;
being children they realize
      that they are the only restitution.
for centuries they have seen the airplanes
        buzzing through their dreams,
      the candy growing like corn nubs
    through turf that replaces their teeth.
having suffered through all this
      the walruses that swim out of the Orient
           and eat them alive, their women
  running from the tents to offer them shucks
in welcome, they wake half in joy
      half in despair and propped in the wind
moving the ice stare in the distance at their feet
    trapped in the boots, white captains
  who decided to go down with their ships.

Wrapped in blankets
                 and linoleum
the peasants tear down the dead
       branches
pulling sledges loaded with samovars
             and birthday cakes behind them
while their children run through the trees
            like ducks.
singing they drag and push the great
       nests, the piles of graves home through the woods.
and after supper sit
                 potato hands
      before them
      making whistles,
         alpine castles with waterwheels
      and running brooks,
and a girl that when you
              push a button
    she leaps from the bathtub,
          steam pouring from her
               ears and nipples.

For the Sierra Club

When they murmur against us
their whispers are battleships.
after the party we find
we have their coats on
that bristle and keep us warm and fit so well.
that driving home graves
have already been dug along the highway.
nevertheless we run with the antelope
in the furniture that leap from the
scorched grain and fruit.
though in winter stranded in the front yard
beneath the stars our hands spread
like petals of frost. and across the neighborhood
we hear the purr of the sleek car bringing
that great dame to the celebration,
who emerges long after hours
sweeping up the stairs, slightly
drunk and carrying her own drink.

The Eskimo Mask

One eye slides down
to the mouth.
in that hole, the shape
of frightened love

you can see the shiny backs
of copper ants
like money at work,
the rotten flesh moving,
digesting itself.

out on the plains on the evening
of the first frost
the moss crushed by your steps,
the winter rooted in your lungs

it is he gliding behind
who stops when you stop
and continues, hands
feelers in the thin air,
round mouth saying
something invisible.

Options

After a while even the things he loves
aren't enough.
like threatened conspirators the trees
give up their secrets,
and the pigs that run around him at sunset
with hairy faces grow so thin
they disappear, like commas, into culverts.

he walks into the desert mountains,
up washes burnt through them.
above all they cry for is more water
so they can eat one another;
from the final peak in the recess
the last goat, with a clock bubbling in his forehead,
waves with the arm sewn to his shoulder.

he knows he must do something.
and there finds a dead locomotive
with writing scribbled over its boiler,
days later comes stumbling into the date shop
skin gone to leather, an arrow in his back,
demands to see a reporter. the stars
have done it and shows the marks over his wrist.

divorces his wife. in Chicago
hacks a secretary to pieces. spends
the rest of his life at the edge
of the continent growing thin, a board
tied to the top of his head, a mirror
tied under his chin, devouring girl swimmers,
counting the waves coming in from
that other land which he sees at times
under the right conditions, beaten by foam, throwing
up its green arms.

El Mozo

A waiter depends on his hearing
if he leaning like an otter on the bristles
                                    of his moustache
toward the lips of the silver cripple
in a wheelchair, who says
                    Queso, Queso, as if speaking of fire
the little pea goes round and round
            down the smooth labyrinth of his ear,
                            gallery without pictures
and hurrying back sped on the
                    shiny bulbs of his feet
to deliver the glue-smeared plastic
            fuselage of an airplane from his fingers
stands back, he knows looking as she looks
                that is not what she will eat
                                    while the gauchos
            strain toward heaven with their teeth.
all night it goes that way with particulars
        corsages melt through the walls
                like bleeding warts,
while he must walk through
            the clothes of waitresses
            shadows of dogs eating the sun,
the necklace found, a spoon
            with the fatal obscene picture on it
                            in the last of the soup
    the heirloom that after all these generations
            the party discovers him, a stranger, wearing.
until they have labored through their sets
            Así Te Quiero, No Te Creas, Día Tras Día
        a moon jogging through its phases
        and they lie on the stage, empty banana skins
and he can run out at 3 A.M. behind
                    his swelling bloody hands
                            guilty with beeves

his head a salad threatening to flame
to the dumb girl who rises naked from the ashcan
and behind her the watery breeze of Lucero
slipping toward him.

Bombs

The biscuits begin bursting
through the sides of the cars
and the engineers seeing them
at midnight like the blue tails
of comets swiping their eyes
start diving to left and right from the train
meet and become brothers stumbling
through the moonless desert swamp
holding their wounds toward the bearded
sleeping St. David. meanwhile behind
the firetrucks have arrived speeding
from all parts of the nation to stand
amazed, hands before their faces at
the volcano sinking into itself,
pulling the white ground and crackling brush,
the phosphorus skin of a new pudding with it
and the soldiers from Fort Huachuca looking grim
buckle their snorkels on. while the two
of them arms around each other
push out their windy baggy legs toward
the bull that blinking over his shoulder
moves off, their heads now
paper bags, two smiling lanterns, and
fifty-eight long cars away, just
entering Bowie the crewmen in the
caboose surround the wedding cake, better
than a woman, raise their musty thumbs
in a toast to each other, feeling the tug.

Poem for Lee Oler

The Hopis told you, stretching out their arms
that if a light should appear at dusk
at the end of the field,
three men in the iron sights of the furrows,
next day your dog will be run over by a truck
in the hogan a fork will fall to the floor.

you have taken all the precautions
and added some, leading the deaf children
through the stores by their stiff elbows,
giving the blind music lessons, who step up
one by one in wooden shoes to try the treasured flute.
and now you say you have seen it,
first pointed out on vacation by your father,
through the binoculars a stone pimple
on the desert mountains that formed a blob,
rose, and drifted off like the buttocks of a star, not
when we ask, beckoning to follow, but
that night felt magnetized to the spot
as if a handsome man were breathing over your shoulder.
next day all had headaches and problems with their bowels.

and now after all the postage like pins
in an apple, bristles growing from a rock
we shake off the casts from our arms
as if they were spiders, signatures made of wire.
you wear a brown wire hat. below my legs
I have my paper bags on. and though
the officers even at this late hour
are in their catacombs stringing their fingers,
their great machines that shouldn't fly

rise from the sea, take off. though
tonight a dog hangs in the back yard
you unscrew a leg and play a tune for us.

Mechanics Dreaming of Africa

All day they stand in the cold barn
the wind a water around their knees
swinging their wrenches, joking
about the Mexican heat, as the locomotives
shuffle toward them, coughing emphysemiacs. like
natives they go right to the heart
mounting the elephants, stripping away the fat,
plunging their tools down to touch
the fist fluttering in blubber;

                                  call up cursing through
the swirling steam and stench for more light.
they swagger through the noon in their bloody pants,
knocking each other into streets, looking once
spit at their reflections in plate glass.
marvelously down on a knee one reaches up the back
of a girl's legs, and comes out as she blinks with
a steaming apple that they toss around.
at night while they sleep mouths open
buffalo hair grows thick across their fingers.
is it any wonder then that they know what heaven is,
recognize in the heads of their dervish children
aquariums with swimming fish, the dream,
as a doctor taking up his saw
considers a baby's skull for autopsy.
or all day they smell it from the market,
on the wind across the ocean, the faint warmth
of bananas, that enormous woman which tools
dangling they can get just one leg around.